Junior World Explorers

Ponce De León

by Wyatt Blassingame
illustrated by Russ Hoover

Chelsea Juniors
A division of Chelsea House Publishers
New York ▪ Philadelphia

THE ASTROLABE, an instrument developed by the Greeks, is the symbol for JUNIOR WORLD EXPLORERS. At the time of Columbus, sailors used the astrolabe to chart a ship's course. The arm across the circle could be moved to line up with the sun or a star. Using the number indicated by the pointer, a sailor could tell his approximate location on the sea. Although the astrolabe was not completely accurate, it helped many early explorers in their efforts to conquer the unknown.

Cover Illustration: Tony Limuaco

First Chelsea House edition 1991

7 9 8

ISBN   0-7910-1493-2

Contents

1

From Page to Squire

The boy stood looking out of the castle window. In the courtyard below him two squires practiced fighting with swords. The master-at-arms stood close by, giving instructions. It was a cold morning. The boy could see the breath of the swordsmen.

Behind the boy a voice said, "Juan!"

He turned swiftly. "I am sorry, Don Pedro. I—"

"You were daydreaming," said Don Pedro Núñez de Guzmán, "while I am freezing."

The boy hurried across the room to the huge fireplace. Don Pedro's clothing was hung on racks in front of the fire. The boy picked up the long hose. Kneeling in front of Don Pedro's chair, he helped the knight put them on. He brought Don Pedro's doublet and boots. "Would you have your breakfast served here, My Lord?"

Don Pedro shook his head. He crossed to the window and looked out. "So," he said. "I see what you were watching, Juan Ponce de León. And I think I know what you were thinking."

Above his dark beard Don Pedro's lips were smiling, but his eyes were serious. "You were thinking that it is high time

you were outside learning to be a soldier. You do not want to be in here helping me get dressed."

"Sir, I—"

Don Pedro laughed aloud. "You were wondering why you must learn to be a servant before you learn to be a soldier. You were wondering why you must polish my armor and sword, when all you want is a sword of your own."

That was exactly what young Juan Ponce de León had been thinking. He blushed, and Don Pedro said, "I know, because that is what every page your age wonders. Yet this is our custom. The sons of knights—like you, Juan—are sent to the homes of other knights for training. That training starts at the bottom. You cannot be a knight unless you are first a page, then a squire.

You have to learn discipline and self-sacrifice, as well as how to use your sword."

Don Pedro paused. His face was very serious now. He said, "At least that is the ideal. It does not always work out that way."

"I am not sure I understand your meaning, My Lord."

"I mean that not all knights are as knightly as we might wish. It is something you will understand better—too well, perhaps—when you grow up." He smiled again. "Right now you are thinking that you must hurry and grow up to be a soldier. You are afraid the wars will be over."

"You do not think so?"

"We Spaniards have been fighting the Moors for over 700 years. If we do not fight the Moors, we fight one another. With us war is a way of life. We know no other. But," he waved his hand, "it does no good to talk to a boy about the future. Boys are interested in the present. And I think you are right, Juan. It is time you began your military training."

Juan's eyes grew big. "You mean—?"

"I mean you should go now and call Ramón. Tell him that from now on he will serve my breakfast. Then go to the master-at-arms. Tell him you are now a full-time student."

"Ye-es . . ." Juan's voice bobbled with excitement. Then he remembered what Don Pedro had said about discipline. He swallowed and said, "Yes, My Lord." He made his feet walk until he was out of the room. Then he ran.

2

A Soldier with No War

Juan Ponce de León learned his lessons well from the master-at-arms. He became an excellent soldier. He and Don Pedro Núñez fought battle after battle against the Moors. The Moors were Arabs from North Africa. They had invaded Spain more than 700 years before Juan was born. Ever since then the Spanish had been fighting to recapture their homeland. Little by little they were winning.

The war against the Moors was not the only war in Spain. Most of the country was divided into small states. They often fought against each other. But as Juan grew up these civil wars ended. The Spanish states became united under Queen Isabella and King Ferdinand. In 1492 the last Moors surrendered. After centuries of fighting, Spain was at peace.

Juan was a young man now. He was married. He was a good soldier, but his country no longer needed soldiers. The Ponce de Leóns were a fine family, but Juan himself was poor. And now he had no job.

Doña Inez, Juan's wife, was worried. "What are you going to do, Juan?" she asked.

He shook his head. "I don't know. I'll think of something."

Suddenly, in 1493, all Spain was excited by strange and wonderful news. The year before, a man named Columbus had sailed off into the Atlantic Ocean. He had been trying to find a new route to India. Now he had returned with stories of unknown islands in the far west. Perhaps these islands were part of India. Nobody knew for sure.

Columbus and his sailors told of finding friendly red-skinned people who thought the white men were gods. They also told of gold and precious jewels. With every telling the stories got wilder and wilder. Soon they were about mountains of gold and diamonds as big as a man's head.

Juan heard the stories. He heard that Columbus was planning a second voyage. Columbus would need trained soldiers to go with him.

Juan talked it over with Doña Inez. "If you went, you would be gone such a long, long time," she said.

"I know." Juan loved his wife. He hated to leave her. At the same time, the idea of going to a new world excited him.

"Do you really believe those stories, Juan? Do you really think that you can pick up gold like rocks along the rivers?"

Juan knew how soldiers and sailors tell tall tales. Still, there must be some truth in what they said. "I will be working for Spain," he said. "If I don't find gold, I will at least have my pay."

It was not as easy to get the job with Columbus as Juan had thought. On Columbus' first voyage almost nobody had wanted to go with him. Now almost everybody wanted to go. There were many soldiers like Juan, out of work with no war to fight.

However, Juan had made a good name for himself as a soldier. His friend Don Pedro was also a friend of the King. He recommended Juan. Soon word came. Juan was to report to a ship in the Bay of Cadiz.

There was a lump in Juan's throat as he kissed Doña Inez good-by. She was crying. Juan almost wished he had never heard of Christopher Columbus or a New World. Still, it was too late to turn back now.

He swung into the saddle and rode toward the coast.

Seventeen ships and more than 1200 men were to make this second voyage with Columbus. On the morning of September 25, 1493, the fleet put to sea.

It was a beautiful morning. A light wind rippled the Bay of Cadiz. The rising sun glowed on the brightly colored sails and on the white walls of the city. Around the fleet sailed many smaller boats. On some of these, musicians were playing. Banners flew. Cannons boomed from ships and shore.

Juan Ponce de León stood on the deck of his ship. His heart beat fast with

excitement. He stared ahead, toward the
vast, open sea that lay between him and
the New World. What would he find
there? A fortune in gold? Death at the
hands of some unknown savage? Both
of these? He could not know.

In the open sea the waves swelled high.
Suddenly Juan had something else to
think about. Was he going to be seasick?
After all, he was a soldier, not a sailor.

3

The New World

The fleet sailed southwest, the ships close together. As far as Juan could see, the sky was filled with their sails. Night after night their lights twinkled like big stars above the dark water.

The morning of November 3 Juan was awakened by the sound of running feet. Then he heard a man shout, *"Tierra!* Land!" Then another voice, and another, "Tierra! Tierra!"

Juan leaped from his hammock. There was no time to put on his clothes. He raced on deck with all the others. The sun was not yet up, but light was spreading across the sky. Overhead Juan could see the masts of the ship. A man was clinging to the rigging with one hand while he pointed with the other. "Tierra!"

Juan saw it then—a low mountain rising out of the sea. As he stared, the rays of the sun touched the mountaintop. Big clouds hung over it, rose-colored in the early light.

As the sun rose higher, more and more islands came into view. "Which one of them is Hispaniola?" Juan asked a sailor. Hispaniola was an island Columbus had discovered on his first voyage. Columbus had left a party of men there when he went back to Spain. It is the island on which Haiti and the Dominican Republic are today.

"Hispaniola is not among these islands," the sailor told Juan. "We are south of Hispaniola. No European has ever seen these islands before."

Juan was anxious to reach Hispaniola. Some of the sailors had been there with Columbus. They said gold could be picked up along the rivers. They had not picked it up themselves. But they had seen a few Indians wearing gold ornaments. They were sure gold must be plentiful.

"I wish I had been one of the men left on Hispaniola," a sailor told Juan. "The men were to hunt for gold. By now they should have a shipload of it."

Finally the fleet reached the eastern

end of Hispaniola. It was a big island. The town of Navidad, where the men had been left, was still some distance away. Before reaching it, Columbus stopped. He sent soldiers ashore to find a place for the new town he planned to build.

Juan did not go with these soldiers, but he heard their story. They found the bodies of two dead Spaniards, tied with ropes. There was no way to tell who had killed them.

"It wouldn't have been the Indians," a sailor said. "They were very friendly. I think our men got to fighting among themselves. Probably it was over the gold."

The fleet hurried on to Navidad. It arrived just at dark. The entrance to the harbor was narrow. Columbus did not want to take his ships through it at night. So he ordered the anchors dropped. Cannons were fired to let the Spaniards on the shore know Columbus had returned.

Juan stood at the rail of his ship. Like everyone else, he waited to hear the boom of answering cannons.

There was the sound of waves lapping against the ship, the cry of a night bird. Nothing else.

Lights were hung in the rigging of all the ships. Surely the men ashore would see them and make some answer. But the shore stayed dark and quiet.

All around Juan men were asking, "What could have happened?"

"Perhaps they found more gold in another part of the island and moved there," one man said.

"Perhaps they died of sickness."

"Perhaps the Indians . . ."

The night passed without answer.

Early next day Juan and other soldiers went ashore with Admiral Columbus. The Admiral led them to where the small fort had been. Now the roof was gone, and the walls broken in. In some bushes nearby lay several dead Spaniards. All the others had disappeared.

It was a long time before Juan and the other soldiers learned what had happened. It was a terrible story.

The men Columbus had left had not obeyed his orders. They had not treated the Indians kindly. Instead, they made slaves of them. They robbed the Indians of what little gold they could find. Too lazy to grow their own food, they took it by force from the Indians.

Finally one of the chiefs rebelled. He

and some of his warriors attacked the fort at night. They killed several of the Spaniards. They drove others into the sea where they were drowned. When the fighting was over not a white man was left alive on the island.

Yet these had been gentle and friendly Indians when treated kindly.

Juan remembered something Don Pedro had said. "Not all knights are as knightly as we might wish." Juan was beginning to understand what Don Pedro meant.

4

Governor of Puerto Rico

When Columbus landed, the Indians who had killed the Spaniards fled to the mountains and hid. The Indians who stayed behind were as friendly as Juan had been told. They shared their food and their houses with the white men. They gave the soldiers what little gold they could find in return for cheap bells and beads.

Juan liked to talk with the Indians. Before long he spoke their language better than most of the Spanish did.

Many of the soldiers did not want to learn the Indians' language. They did not want to plant crops and build houses. "Make the Indians raise food for us," they said. "Make them build our houses and find gold for us."

It was gold the Spanish wanted most. However, there was really very little gold on the island. Even this little bit was hard to find. To get it, the Spanish made the Indians work as slaves. But no matter how hard the Indians worked, they could not get much gold. This made the Spanish angry. They punished the Indians by whipping them or by cutting off their ears.

Finally, even those Indians who had

been peaceful began to fight back. It was an uneven fight. The Indians had no armor or swords of steel. Their bows were not as good as the Spanish cross-bows. They had no cannons. Within a few years more than half the Indians on Hispaniola had been killed. Some hid in the mountains. They would rather starve than work for the Spanish. Those who did surrender lived like slaves.

Juan Ponce de León was a soldier. He fought the Indians along with the others.

Many of the soldiers decided to return to Spain. They were disappointed because there was so little gold. But Juan liked this lush green country where it was always warm. He wanted to make his home here.

Juan sent for Doña Inez to join him. For awhile they lived in a small house in the new town of Santo Domingo. Here their first child, a little girl, was born. Juan was very proud of her.

New settlers and soldiers came to Hispaniola from Spain. Juan was made captain of all the soldiers in Santo Domingo. He led them in battles against the Indians of Higuey. This was a section close to the eastern end of Hispaniola. When the Higuey Indians were defeated, Juan was made Lieutenant Governor of the area. He was given a large plantation and many slaves.

It was a new kind of life for Juan, with no battles to fight. He built a handsome white home for Doña Inez and the children. He had three daughters now, and a son. Juan loved them all. He found life in Higuey very pleasant.

One day Juan saw an Indian wearing

a large, flat piece of gold on a cord around his neck. It was bigger than any other piece of gold Juan had seen in Hispaniola. "Where did you find it?" he asked.

The Indian pointed toward the east. "Borinquen."

Borinquen was the Indian name for an island Columbus had named San Juan Bautista. Today it is called Puerto Rico. It was only a day's sail from Hispaniola, but no Spaniards had ever explored it. "Is there much gold on this island?" Juan asked the Indian.

The Indian spread his hands. "Very much."

Juan did not know whether or not to believe him. The Indians often pointed toward far off places and said gold could be found there. They hoped the

Spanish would then go away to search for the gold, and leave them in peace.

Juan took the Indian's gold. He showed it to Don Nicolás de Ovando, the new Governor of Hispaniola. "There is only one way to know if the Indian told the truth," Don Nicolás said. "You must go and find out. Even if there is no gold, the land may be rich. If you find gold, or good land to farm, I will make you governor."

With a party of soldiers, Juan sailed for Puerto Rico. "The Indians there do not know us," Juan told his men. "If we make friends of them, we can trade with them. They will give us gold in return for cheap bells and beads. They will plant crops and tend cattle for low wages. If we make enemies of them, there will be fighting. We would win,

but these Indians do not make good slaves. Many had rather die than work as slaves. So it is better for everybody to be friends."

The Indians on Puerto Rico were as friendly to Juan as those on Hispaniola had been to Columbus. The Chief's name was Guaybana. He and Juan became close friends. Guaybana showed Juan rivers in which there really was some gold. There were not large amounts, but there was more than had been found in Higuey. There was also rich soil for raising crops.

Juan reported to Governor Ovando what he had found. Ovando made him Governor of Puerto Rico. Juan took soldiers and settlers to found a colony. His family was among them.

Juan's men were under strict orders to

treat the Indians kindly. So they all lived in peace. The Indians helped with the crops. They helped search for gold. As governor, Juan got part of everything the island produced. He began to grow rich.

But suddenly everything was changed. King Ferdinand sent a new governor to replace Ovando. The new governor was Don Diego Columbus, the son of the Admiral Christopher Columbus. Don Diego appointed two friends of his own, Juan Ceron and Miguel Diaz, to rule Puerto Rico.

Once more Juan Ponce de León was out of a job. He returned to Hispaniola.

5

Indian Uprising

Juan was a rich man now. He did not need to work. He could go back to Spain, if he wished. But he and his wife and children all liked the New World.

While Juan tried to decide what to do, his friend Ovando returned to Spain. Ovando told King Ferdinand that Juan was the best man to be Governor of Puerto Rico. So just as suddenly as he had lost his job, Juan had it back again.

He found things very changed. Ceron and Diaz had treated the Indians cruelly. As a result, the Indians were no longer friendly.

Juan's first order was to have Ceron and Diaz arrested. But it was too late to prevent trouble with the Indians.

One morning Juan was eating his breakfast when he heard men shouting. The door opened and a wounded soldier staggered into the room. Gasping for breath, he told Juan a Spanish village had been attacked. "It was the middle of the night. Almost everyone was asleep," he said. "Many were killed in their beds, women and children as well as soldiers. I managed to escape. But on the way here I was forced to hide many times. Everywhere the Indians are beating their war drums and blowing their conch-shell

horns. The other towns are sure to be attacked."

Quickly Juan sent messengers to all the Spanish villages on the islands. Everyone was to come to Caparra, where Juan lived. Here the women and children would be safer. And with all his soldiers together, Juan would have a better chance of defeating the Indians.

Even so, Juan had less than 100 soldiers. The Indians would outnumber him ten to one. He sent a ship to Hispaniola asking for more soldiers.

Then he divided his men into three groups. One group at a time would attack the Indians, then quickly retreat into Caparra. These attacks kept the Indians so busy, they could not make a big attack of their own.

One of Juan's best soldiers was a big,

vicious dog named Berezillo. Berezillo was trained to catch Indians by the throat and kill them. The Indians had never seen horses or savage dogs before the Spanish came. They believed such animals were devils. Whenever Berezillo rushed at an Indian, the Indians nearby would turn and run.

After a few days soldiers arrived from Hispaniola. Although Juan's troops were still far outnumbered, he decided to begin the attack.

The two armies met in a large valley. The Spanish horsemen charged. The Indians were terrified of the horses. They broke and ran. At the same time, however, other Indians attacked from other directions. Soon the small Spanish army was completely surrounded.

The Spanish guns and crossbows would

shoot farther than the bows of the
Indians. Spanish armor stopped many of
the Indian arrows. Even so, many of the
Spanish were killed. And the Indians
kept coming.

One Indian chief led the attack. Time
after time he and his warriors rushed
the Spanish. Each time the Indians were
beaten back. Each time they charged

again. Then a Spanish arrow struck the chief. When he fell, the Indians with him stopped fighting.

Quickly Juan ordered his horsemen to charge. This time all the Indians broke and ran. Without their leader they were no longer an organized army. Juan's men had only to catch the Indians one at a time to kill or capture them.

Shortly after this another letter arrived from King Ferdinand. Once more the King had changed his mind. Don Diego had been angry when Juan had arrested friends. He had complained to the King. Once again Ceron and Diaz were to govern Puerto Rico. And once again Juan was out of a job.

6

A Letter from the King

Juan did not want to stay in Puerto Rico now that Ceron and Diaz were in command. He did not want to go to Hispaniola where his enemy, Don Diego Columbus, was governor. Nor did he want to go back to Spain. Once more he and Doña Inez talked over the future.

"What I would like most," Juan said, "is to have two or three ships. I have money enough. I could buy them myself. Then I could go exploring. Columbus discovered these islands and many others to the south and west. But certainly there is land to the northwest as well."

"You mean Bimini?" Doña Inez asked.

"The Indians all say there is an island called Bimini. They tell of other land to the northwest also."

Doña Inez touched her slightly graying hair. "Juan, do you believe that story about the Fountain of Youth?"

Juan Ponce knew the story. The Indians on Hispaniola and Puerto Rico both told it. Even the fierce Carib Indians to the south knew the story. On the island of Bimini, the story said, there was a large spring. A river ran from it. If an old man or woman drank the water and bathed in the river, he or she was made young again. None of the Indians who told the story had ever been to Bimini. But they had all heard of somebody who had heard of somebody who had been there.

"Do you believe that story?" Doña Inez asked again.

"I don't know," Juan said. "Years ago I heard that Columbus was trying to find India by sailing west. I didn't believe it was possible." He paused. "I still don't know if this new world is part of India or not. Nobody does. So I don't know what I may find. If there is no magic fountain, there may be gold. There may be rich farming land. Whatever I find, Don Diego won't be the governor."

Doña Inez smiled. "Now I can see why

you want to go. But don't you need permission from the King to do this?"

"I will write him a letter and ask," Juan said.

Nobody knows just what was in the letter Juan wrote to the King. Certainly he mentioned Bimini. But we do not know if he said anything about a Fountain of Youth.

The King wrote to Juan:

"I grant you permission to go and discover and settle the island of Bimini . . ."

Quickly Juan set out to buy and equip three ships. Since he was a soldier, not a sailor, he wanted to hire the best sailor he could find as pilot. The man he got was named Anton de Alaminos, an excellent navigator. Together Juan and Alaminos hired soldiers and sailors to

make the voyage. They began carefully to fill the ships with supplies.

Suddenly Juan got a second letter from the King. It ordered him to come to Spain in a hurry, *"Because I want to learn from you something important . . . to me. Having come here I will order what you must do."*

We do not know what made the King order Juan back to Spain in such a hurry. Ferdinand was 60. Perhaps he had heard the story of the magic fountain of Bimini and wanted to ask Juan about it. Perhaps he wanted to make sure that Juan's voyage did not get Spain in trouble with other countries. He may have wanted to tell Juan what to do with any gold he might find. We do not know.

We do not even know for sure that

Juan went to see the King. Probably he did. If so, he was soon back in Puerto Rico. His three ships, the *Santa Maria de Consolación*, the *Santiago*, and the *San Cristoval* were ready to sail.

Juan's family came to the wharf to see him off. His children were all in their teens now. His son was the youngest. "I wish I could go with you," he said.

Juan put his hand on his son's shoulder. "Next time, perhaps."

"Perhaps we can all go, if you really find Bimini," Doña Inez said.

A small boat took Juan to where the *Santa Maria* lay at anchor. He climbed aboard and waved to his family. The ship's anchor was raised. Sails flashing in the sun, the *Santa Maria*, the *San Cristoval*, and the *Santiago* left the harbor.

It was the afternoon of March 3, 1513.

7

La Florida

A few days after leaving Puerto Rico, Juan's ships reached the island of San Salvador. This was the first island Columbus had discovered in the New World. From it Columbus had sailed southwest. The bows of Juan's ships pointed northwest. Soon he was in waters where no white man had been before.

Day after day the ships sailed across an empty sea. To the west, just out of sight, were the hundreds of islands we call the Bahamas. Neither Juan nor Alaminos knew this. They held steady to their course.

March 27 was Easter Sunday. The Spanish called Easter the "Feast of Flowers," or *Pascua Florida*. Juan had brought no priests on the voyage, but the men on the ships held services. The services were barely over when the lookout on Juan's ship cried, "Tierra!"

Quickly Juan climbed into the rigging to get a better view. There was only a small spot on the horizon. He called to the sailor in the crow's nest, "What does it look like to you?"

"An island. A very small island."

Anton de Alaminos, the pilot, was not

on the same ship with Juan. Alaminos was aboard the *Santiago*. The sailor in command of Juan's ship was named Don Bono de Quejo. Juan turned to him. "What do you think, Captain?"

"It seems to be very small. Bimini is supposed to be bigger."

"That's how it looks to me," Juan said. "Signal to Captain Alaminos and to the other ship that we will not stop."

Probably the land Juan saw on Easter Sunday was Man of War Cay, one of the Bahama islands.

Three days later the ships ran into a storm. The wind blew hard all one day and night. Dark-blue waves tossed the ships like chips of wood. Alaminos, the pilot, changed course. Now the ships sailed west northwest.

The storm ended. The sea became

calm. It was the second of April, 1513. Once more the man in the crow's nest shouted, "Tierra!"

Soon all the men could see land. It lay in a long, low line ahead of them. As the ships moved toward it, the water became more shallow. Alaminos signaled from the *Santiago* not to go closer. He was afraid of running aground.

Juan signaled back to turn north. They would search for a harbor.

Carefully the ships moved along the coast. They were close enough now for Juan to see a long, silver line of beach. Behind it the trees were dark green. There were no mountains, not even hills. An offshore wind brought the smell of growing things.

"It is a large island," Captain Quejo said to Juan.

"And a very pretty one."

"Do you think it is Bimini?"

"There are supposed to be hills on Bimini," Juan replied.

"If it is not Bimini, you must give it a name," Captain Quejo said.

Juan looked thoughtfully at the land. Like Captain Quejo he believed that what he had found was an island. He had found it in the Easter season, *la Pascua Florida*, the time of the "Feast of Flowers." From here the land looked as though it might be full of flowers.

"I will call it *la Florida*," Juan said.

Some historians believe that an Italian explorer named John Cabot sailed along the Florida coast fifteen years before Juan Ponce. Some believe the Norsemen went there 500 years before. It is possible. Nobody knows for sure. We do know, however, that the written history of what is now the United States of America starts with that bright April 2, 1513. It starts with Juan Ponce de León looking thoughtfully toward the green and silver land, and saying, "I will call it Florida."

The land still bears the name he gave it.

8

Sailing Backward

Juan's ships moved slowly along the coast. Night came and they had not found a harbor. Alaminos, the pilot, ordered the ships to anchor and wait for morning.

Probably it was early on the next morning, the sun still low over the Atlantic, when Juan first went ashore. Exactly where this landing was made, we do not know. But it was close to where St. Augustine stands today. Juan claimed the land for Spain. Then he and his men went looking for Indians. He wanted to ask questions about this new land he had discovered. He also wanted to ask the way to Bimini.

He found no Indians. If any lived close by, they had seen the ships and hidden in fear. Juan found fresh water, but it did not make him any younger. After a few days he sailed again, going north up the coast.

This time he went north for only one day. Then he turned south again. If he had gone only a few more miles north, he would have found the mouth of the big river we call the St. Johns. He would have known from its size that what he had discovered was not an island.

Instead, he turned south just before reaching the river.

For twelve days the ships moved down the coast. Then Juan saw an Indian village. He sent some soldiers ashore to explore. They found the village deserted, the Indians gone.

The next day Juan was leaning against the ship's rail when Captain Quejo came to him. Beneath his beard the Captain's face was chalky white. His dark eyes looked frightened. "A very strange thing is happening," he said. "I just cannot understand it."

"What do you mean?" Juan asked.

"Look at the shore."

Juan saw a white beach with trees beyond it. "It looks like the shore we have been following."

"Yes. Now look at the sails."

The sails were filled with a strong north wind. It drove the ship swiftly through the water. "We are sailing very fast," Juan said.

"So I thought. But now look at the shore again. Watch that tall tree ahead."

Juan did. His forehead began to wrinkle in a frown. The tree ahead was not getting closer. Instead it was getting farther away. He looked at the sails again. They were still filled with wind. Yet instead of going ahead, the three ships were actually sailing backward.

"But why?" Juan asked. "What is happening?"

At this moment signal flags began to flutter from the mast of Alaminos' ship. "He is ordering us to anchor!" Captain Quejo cried. He ran forward, shouting his own orders.

The anchor went down with a clatter. The *Santa Maria* pulled against it like a horse trying to run away. One of the other ships had also anchored. The third ship was farther from shore and its anchor chain would not reach bottom. Its sails were filled with a wind that should be driving it southward. But the ship moved steadily backward, to the north. Gradually it disappeared from sight.

"There must be a very great current here," Captain Quejo told Juan. "I have spent many years at sea and met many ocean currents. I have met nothing like this one."

It was the Spaniards' first adventure with the Gulf Stream. This great current flows like a vast river around the southern tip of Florida. Then it flows northward up the Atlantic. Juan's ships had crossed it while sailing toward Florida. But that crossing had been mostly at night and during a storm. Busy with the storm, they had not realized they were being carried north.

"What will the ship do that was carried away?" Juan asked.

"This current does not flow near shore," Captain Quejo said. "If the Captain takes his ship closer to land, he can sail southward again."

"Then we must wait for him," Juan said.

Just then the sailor in the crow's nest called out, "Indians on the beach, Captain. They are waving for us to come ashore."

9

War with the
Indians

Juan had been looking for Indians to talk with. He wanted to ask if gold could be found in this land he had discovered. Was the soil good for farming? In which direction was the island of Bimini?

Quickly he ordered a small boat put over the side of the *Santa Maria*. With a few of his soldiers, he was rowed toward the shore. On the beach a crowd of Indians was shouting and waving. Some had bows and arrows, some clubs, some spears.

"Keep your weapons ready," Juan told his men. "But start no trouble. Let us hope these people are as peaceful as the Indians in Hispaniola when we first went there."

"Do you think they have heard what happened to those Indians?" a soldier said. "They might not want us here."

The answer came quickly. As the boat touched ground, the Indians rushed toward it. Some of them tried to take the oars away from the sailors. Some tried to pull the boat onto the beach so it could not get away. One Indian grabbed at Juan's sword, another at his shield.

At first there were no blows. The

Spaniards struggled to hold onto their
arms. The Indians tried to take them.
Then, suddenly, an Indian raised his war
club and brought it down on the head of
a sailor. The sailor fell, unconscious.

Quickly the Spanish drew their swords.
The Indians jumped out of reach. There
was the sharp twang of bowstrings, and
two more Spaniards fell, badly wounded.

From the *Santa Maria*, Captain Quejo could see what was happening. He ordered a cannon fired. The shot did not hit any of the Indians, but the boom frightened them. They raced across the beach and hid in the tall grass. From there they kept firing arrows. The shields of the Spanish protected them until their boat was out of range.

Next day, the ship which had been carried away by the Gulf Stream returned. All three ships then fought their way south around a point of land. Juan named it the Cape of Currents. This may have been what we now call Cape Canaveral (or Cape Kennedy), or near the modern city of Palm Beach. The ships kept close to shore to avoid the Gulf Stream. They passed where Miami is now. They sailed along the little islands called the Florida Keys. At the end of the Keys, the ships turned north again. Once more they reached the mainland of Florida, this time the west coast. Here in a quiet bay, Alaminos anchored to repair some worm-eaten planks on the *San Cristoval*.

Juan was in his cabin when a sailor came to him. "There is an Indian who speaks Spanish," the sailor cried. "He wants to talk with you."

"Spanish?" Juan said. "How can an Indian here speak Spanish? Bring him to me."

"He is in a canoe. He won't come on board."

Juan ran on deck. He saw several Indians in a canoe. They were almost an arrow's shot from the ship. "I am Juan Ponce de León, in command of these ships," Juan called out. "Who wants to speak with me?"

An Indian stood up in the canoe. "I come from our great Chief Carlos," he shouted. "He wishes you to stay here. Soon he will come to trade, bringing much gold."

The word "gold" made all the Spanish excited. They had seen none so far.

"I will be glad to see your chief," Juan called. "Come on my ship, I will give you presents for him."

The Indian shook his head. "Chief Carlos will come himself."

"How is it you speak Spanish?" Juan shouted.

The Indian did not answer. Instead he and his companions paddled quickly away.

Captain Quejo had come out on deck. "That Indian must once have lived in Hispaniola," he said. "He must have sailed all the way to this island in a canoe."

"Yes," Juan slowly replied. He added thoughtfully, "Perhaps that explains why all the Indians we have met here have been so warlike. They have heard of what we did in Hispaniola."

Next day a long line of canoes came into the bay. Some of them were tied together so they could not easily turn over. All were filled with warriors. Slowly they moved toward the ships.

Juan had already given orders. His men were to be ready for war or peace. If the Indians really wanted to trade, they would be allowed aboard a few at a time.

Suddenly a cloud of arrows shot from the canoes. Some of the canoes raced to the anchor chains of the Spanish ships. The Indians tried to cut the chains so the ships would drift ashore. Others kept firing arrows.

The Spanish fired back with their crossbows. Armed soldiers leaped into a small boat. With it they rammed some of the canoes and overturned them.

Many Indians were killed swimming in the water. The others fled, and the fight was over. On the Spanish ships one soldier had been killed by an arrow.

This fight may have taken place in what is now Tampa Bay. It may have been near Punta Gorda or Sanibel Island. When it was over Alaminos asked Juan to return to Puerto Rico. "The hurricane season is coming," Alaminos said. "Also, the ships all need repairs. We cannot repair them here and fight Indians at the same time."

"All right," Juan said. He had not discovered any place called Bimini, but he had discovered a new country. "Soon I will come back," he said. "I will bring more people with me. I will start a colony in this new land."

10

Return to Florida

On the way home a hurricane struck
Juan's ships. Two of them were badly
damaged. With these ships Juan sailed
straight for home once the storm was
over. Alaminos was in the undamaged
ship. Juan sent him home by a different
route.

On his way, Alaminos discovered the
island the Indians called Bimini. It was
a pretty island, but it had no gold and

no magic fountain. When he was sure of this, Alaminos sailed to Puerto Rico and told Juan what he had found.

Juan was anxious to return to Florida. First, however, he would need new ships. And he must report to King Ferdinand in Spain.

The King listened with interest to Juan's story. He gave Juan permission to start a colony in Florida. "But first," the King said, "I have another job for you. I want you to conquer the Carib Indians."

The Caribs were cannibals who lived on islands south of Puerto Rico. They were fierce fighters and often raided Puerto Rico to capture Indian slaves. "I'll try," Juan told the King.

It proved to be a very difficult job. The Caribs had learned they could not defeat the Spanish in open battle. Instead, they attacked from hiding, then ran. They slipped at night from one island to the next. Juan was never able to corner and conquer them. But he forced them to stop raiding Puerto Rico.

While Juan was chasing the Caribs, Doña Inez became seriously ill. As soon as he heard this, Juan rushed home. He hired the best doctors in all the New World. But there was nothing anyone could do to help. Doña Inez died.

Juan was overcome with grief. For several years he gave up being a soldier. He stayed home with his children. For a while he forgot all about Florida.

As time passed, Juan's daughters got married. His son moved to Hispaniola and went into business. Left alone, Juan once more began to think about Florida.

He made his plans carefully. He bought horses and cows and goats and pigs to take with him. He got tools to farm the land and seed to plant. He hired farmers and carpenters, as well as soldiers. Some of them took their wives with them.

In February, 1521, he set sail for the west coast of Florida. Probably he went back to the same good harbor where he had found the Indian who spoke Spanish.

When he got there a cold wind was blowing out of the north. The Spanish had brought no warm clothing with them. Instead of clearing land and building houses, they built fires and huddled around them. They grumbled about the weather. Juan knew that the fierce Florida Indians were near. He sent out scouts to guard against a surprise attack.

11

The Last Fight

Juan's scouts must have spent more time trying to keep warm than looking for Indians. For suddenly, without any warning, an attack came.

Juan heard a man shout, a dog bark. In the same moment a swarm of arrows came from the nearby trees. Soldiers and settlers fell wounded. The sudden screams of women mingled with the war whoops of the Indians.

Juan had to shout his orders above the
noise. He formed the soldiers into units.
Families were sent to the ships for safety.

The arrows seemed to come from every
direction. Yet only a few Indians could
be seen. Most were hidden behind trees
and in the tall grass.

"Follow me!" Juan shouted at his

soldiers. He knew the Indians would not fight at close quarters. Their clubs were no match for the swords and armor of the Spaniards. Juan charged with his men toward the trees from which the most arrows came.

The Indians ahead of the soldiers ran deeper into the woods. But from each

side came more arrows. Back and forth
the Spanish rushed. They killed the
Indians they caught. Crossbowmen fired
at those who ran away.

Yet whenever the Indians were forced
from one spot, more came from another.
Juan could only guess at their numbers.

An arrow struck Juan in the thigh. It
drove through his armor and deep into
the bone. The force of the blow knocked
him down, unconscious.

The soldiers near Juan rushed to
protect him. Some of them lifted him up
and carried him toward the beach.

It was several hours before Juan
opened his eyes. He was in his cabin on
the ship. A soldier stood close by. "How
did the fight go?" Juan asked weakly.

"The Indians ran. But they are still
nearby. Our men are on the ships."

"Did we lose many?"

The soldier nodded. "I do not know how many. There were many killed and more wounded, workmen as well as soldiers. I do not think the workmen will want to go ashore again. Also, the Captain thinks you should be taken to Hispaniola as soon as possible. You can get better care there."

Juan started to say no, then stopped. There were many others wounded beside himself. They would need care too. It would be best to go back, for now. He could get more soldiers, new workers, and start over. In a few months he could be back in Florida again. "Very well," he said at last. "Tell the Captain to up anchor."

As the ships sailed south, Juan's wound got worse instead of better. He was feverish most of the time. A storm struck the fleet and the ships became separated. One of them was blown so far off course it landed in Mexico. The ship with Juan docked in Cuba.

Juan was very weak now and in great pain. He knew he could not live. He called in a friend and made his will. Everything left from his voyage was to be sold. The money would be given to his son and daughters. The land he owned in Puerto Rico would be divided among them. With that done he called for a priest. Within a few hours he was dead.

It was June, 1521.

Other Spanish ships would follow Juan Ponce de León to the coast of Florida. Pánfilo de Narváez and Hernando de Soto landed troops there to explore.

Finally another Spaniard, Pedro Menéndez de Avilés, followed the course of Juan's first voyage. He landed close to where Juan had landed, 52 years before. There, in 1565, he started the city of St. Augustine, the oldest city in what is now the United States of America.